Lifting the Turtle

D1547653

Lifting the Turtle

Poems by J.D. Scrimgeour

Turning Point

© 2017 by J.D. Scrimgeour

Published by Turning Point
P.O. Box 541106
Cincinnati, OH 45254-1106

ISBN: 9781625492548

Poetry Editor: Kevin Walzer
Business Editor: Lori Jareo

Visit us on the web at www.turningpointbooks.com

Acknowledgements

Birmingham Poetry Review: "Lifting the Turtle," "Pinecroft Dairy"
Columbia: "Me and Kenneth"
Diner: "The Baby" (excerpts of "The Baby" also appeared on the Massachusetts Cultural Council Finalists webpage)
Drunk Monkeys: "Cell," "Father Bob," "Laid-Off Elementary School Libarian," "Photo of Molly," "Salem, Mass," "Whitman"
Drunken Boat: "Cemetery Poem" (published as "Cemetery")
Ekphrastic Review: "Salem Common"
Ibbetson Street Review: "Blueberries"
Massachusetts Poetry Festival Anthology: "Monarch"
Off the Coast: "Indiana"
Poetry Soup: "After Tu Fu," "In the Months of the Roaches," "My Graveyards," "Wine"
Salamander: "Hardy's Heart"
Thought & Action: "Territory" (excerpts)
ZigZag Folio: "Scene From Abu Ghraib"

"Prayer to My People," "Territory," "Cirinna," and "The Baby" were published in the chapbook, *Territories* (Last Automat Press, 2013).

Thanks to those who read drafts of this manuscript and helped it find its final shape: Eileen FitzGerald, Alan Feldman, Jeffrey Harrison, Claire Keyes, January Gill O'Neil, James and Christine Scrimgeour.

Thanks, too, to Brian Brodeur, MP Carver, Kevin Carey, Kolleen Carney, James Connatser, Kristen Corcoran, Richard Elia, Richard Hoffman, Lis Horowitz, Jennifer Jean, Jennifer Martelli, Colleen Michaels, Anne Noonan, Lou Orfanella, Dawn Paul, Peter Sampieri, Aidan Scrimgeour, Guthrie Scrimgeour, Phil Swanson, Keja Valens, and Cindy Veach.

And a deep thanks to the Salem Writers Group, which has provided stimulation, inspiration and community.

The Salem Athenaeum, the Writers' Room of Boston, and Salem State University provided support and space.

Cover Design: Emily Dunnigan
Cover Photo: Kim Mimnaugh

Table of Contents

for Christine Xanthakos Scrimgeour
and James Richard Scrimgeour,
who know that love is holy.

We know it. We are time.

C. P. Cavafy

I.

Wine

I want my words to be like wine,
pressed from the earth's fruit,
aged and smoothed, tasty
and potent. Something to take in
with other worldly pleasures,
something you'll absorb that stays
within you, that makes you want more,
but not too much more; nothing
to give you a headache, just something
that leaves you mellow and melancholy,
that celebrates and mourns, and sits
on the kitchen table late in the evening,
not your friend, exactly, but what passes
between friends.

The Writer's Retreat

It is all hung by an invisible white hair.
—*Hart Crane, "My Grandmother's Love Letters"*

A few years ago I climbed into my parents' attic
with the wasps and the squirrels and hauled out
the tattered cardboard box of old notebooks
from back when writing gleamed with promise.

There were moments in the notebooks—
lines that seemed exact, an image that leapt
from the faded pages, sparking the fire of memory,
but mainly I was disappointed.

I wasn't asking for much, no proof of genius,
but where, simply, was *me*? That life
I know I lived? I'd see a wisp of the night
we walked a long field of snow to her cabin.

I hear the rumble of drums those protest evenings
when we chained the doors to Hamilton Hall,
and there's the stink of manure from the farm
behind my parents' house.

But most of it—whatever *it* is—was gone.
Goodbye, my life…
                    Inside the box there's a smaller box,
a shoebox of letters: notes from old girlfriends,
the one letter my mother sent—breezy and funny.

And there's a letter my sister sent from Spain—
six pages. I stare at it, remember when I first read it
sitting in that apartment in the middle of Indiana.
She was so deeply in love it scared me.

I wish I had that letter with me now, as I sit
in this former convent, surrounded by books of faith.
I probably wouldn't read it, just smooth the pages.
"Dear J.D.," would be enough.

I remember feeling she'd gotten closer
to who she was than I would ever get.

Monarch

I know it was Time itself,
that butterfly I saw, dead,
on the sidewalk yesterday
as I walked home from my forties

to my house on Winthrop Street
down the block from the cemetery.
I stopped—mid-life—and looked at Time.
I couldn't pass it by—so bright

orange, so deep black, like pupils.
My years had been uneventful:
marriage, sons, a busted knee.
But when I gazed at Time,

and the wind shifted,
fluttering a wing, I saw myself
sobbing at my grandmother's funeral
twenty-two years ago, hugging my sister

to me. An August day,
the heat unbearable in my suit,
and behind my sister's head,
shimmering in the humid breeze,

a butterfly, off, alighting
on a nearby gravestone, then
up again—a flash—gone,
out of my blurry vision—

and now, what I thought was dead
flaps its wings twice and rises,
brushing past my left cheek,
swerving behind my head,

then sailing and clutching over
the Canal Street traffic.

My Graveyards

There's the one in Southbridge,
where my grandparents are buried,

and the one somewhere in Shrewsbury,
where my grandparents are buried.

There's the one Eileen and I walked through
as the sun set over Bloomington.

Hogie Carmichael is buried there.
There's the one that looked over the golf course

where Mr. Zaido, who liked golf,
was buried. There's the one down the block

from my house where the dogs are taken
to shit. And the one near my family's home

in Connecticut, where I sat in a car
and smoked pot. And the one where my Aunt

Jeanne is buried, where my cousin Demetri
tossed some roses from the arrangements

into the grave. Red roses. Oh, and the one
on that long bike ride on country roads,

the Indiana countryside. No more
than 20 headstones. Every date before 1900.

A road hardly traveled, in a county
hardly traveled. Fields, forest, flowers,

and this small old graveyard that someone
had recently mowed.

Cemetery Poem

Sooner or later every poet writes a cemetery poem.
And, in most of them—all, really—there's death.

And life, too—grass growing, or a bird crossing the sky,
maybe some token left from the living for the dead:

a plastic toy from McDonalds, some flowers,
already wilting, a poem copied out on lined paper.

Cemetery poems mention tampons, or feminine hygiene
generally, less frequently. Ditto eggplant.

And it's the rare cemetery poem that celebrates yet deplores
the addictive qualities of the Boggle App.

You almost can't have a cemetery poem
without the word "stone": headstone, gravestone;

and in almost every cemetery poem, even the ones
that try to end by honoring life and the sublime,

there's a whiff of the pointlessness of it all,
the stony silence of non-being.

No wonder Frank O'Hara wrote about juju beans
and kangaroos! Cemetery poems can be depressing,

one-note shit, especially if you toss in the political:
mass graves, some garish anecdote of an atrocity—

dismemberment, rape, etc., which makes it all seem
worse than pointless. The point being suffering and injustice.

Then, there's the macabre, which is just boring,
and the mock-macabre, which may be more boring.

Rarely do cemetery poems battle for airtime
and interrupt each other: *I've known cemetery poems*

and you, my friend, are no cemetery poem.
Cemetery poems might actually be more about poetry

than cemeteries, in which case there's no such thing
as a cemetery poem, just poems about poetry,

but I hope that's not true because if it is,
then every poem is a cemetery.

Cell

If I could, I'd use
my recently purchased cell phone
to call the pay phone outside
the community swimming pool
in Fairview Park, Normal, Illinois,
that summer when I was eleven,
and the country 200.

And I'd have the phone ring
just as I was passing by on my
aqua-colored bike with 24-inch wheels.
I'd also make myself more brave
than I was at eleven.
I'd hop off the bike,
thwack the kickstand down
and answer, "Hello."

And at the other end of the line,
I would probably not be so brave.
I'd hear that eleven-year-old voice
squeak its cusp-of-puberty
"Hello"—so like my own son
on the phone earlier tonight
as I spoke to him from a bedroom
in this creaky farmhouse
two states away from my home—
"Hello." And I would not speak,
listening to my youthful breaths,
imagining me standing there
shirtless, hand on hip,
shouts and splashes behind me
muffled by the humid Illinois air.

No. No words. The keyhole
in the bedroom door lets in
a gem of light from the hall.
“Who—” the boy says, “who is this?”

Housesitting

We were in the famous poet's house,
on his king-size bed, and I was on top.
It was summer. We were young.
The window to the alley was open,
gauzy curtains pulled wide,
and the phone rang; it rang and rang,
so I answered. The neighbor we'd never met
said a man was outside the window,
and I looked over, saw something move.
I walked closer, and he rushed away,
his shoes flopping down the alley.

Windows had been just ways to cool down.
The world was for us, it performed
for *our* pleasure: maples shivering in a storm,
taut apples arrayed in the farmer's market,
the quarry's transparent heart.

In the decades since, I've imagined that man,
his face always hazy, his pants unzipped,
stroking himself watching us.
I'm bracing my arms, the blankets off,
torso arching, her hair and skin
scented with chlorine from her daily swim....
Some things we never do again.

A breeze sways the curtains.
That window. Its finely netted screen.

Lifting the Turtle

Yesterday on the bike path, the moving rock turned out
to be a turtle,

and when my son and I stopped and dropped our bikes
to the grass, it scooted

as fast as a turtle can scoot (I'd guess), taking just
a few seconds

to reach the shelter of the long weeds. But since Guthrie
had never held

a turtle, I pulled it out of its fear into a greater fear,
when I reached down

and lifted it by its shell and held it at my waist.
Oh, its legs

twisted and clawed, its neck extracted and contracted.
It even peed.

(Wouldn't you?) And Guthrie touched its back, then held it,
then set it down

on the edge of the path where it again crawled to safety,
not quite so fast,

as if the panic had run its course, as if the wonder of flight,
the fact

of its own futility in the acts of the gods, had made its life
more full, more divine.

Photo of Molly

Tilted
head, right arm
behind the back, fingers
curled around the left arm's inner
elbow

as if
holding her own
soft self together, or
taking her own pulse. Skin. Clouds.
Braces.

Smiling
on a French road,
seventeen, a year before
her death. Tilted head angling
toward

some blue
corner of the sky,
patched with white clouds, thin
line of skin between shirt and jeans,
hips wide

as if
having given
birth already, tilted
hips, and, beside them, dangling, her
left hand

open
fingers stretching
upward, as if holding
the warm day delicately
open.

My Father's Rages (With Comment By My Mother)

In his rare and tepid rages,
my father would say "Enough,"
slam the front door,
and disappear for thirty minutes,
walking the circle of our block.

He never hit anyone. I can't
imagine him ever hitting anyone.
When he was in the army, stationed
in Germany between wars,
he didn't get loaded or laid.

He'd stay in the barracks and play chess,
or read Nietzche and Camus.
After golfing with his brother-in-laws,
he'd order a milkshake while they drank beers.
They called him "Mr. Softee."

Until now, I've never thought of his walk
through the neighborhood, past the Malloys',
whose kids were too stupid to play with,
past the road that led to McDonalds,
past the farm bordering the subdivision,

along the street—there were no sidewalks—
his pace slowing, sweat drying beneath his shirt
until it's just an evening stroll,
until, standing again in front of our house,
he stops completely.

He removes his glasses, wipes
his sleeve across his forehead,
puts the glasses back on, fingers
pressing them into place,
and gazes at Jerusalem Hill,

that small mountain with firs,
oak and maple, that rises behind the house.
The quarrel between him and my mother
has blown like a breeze over that mountain
he's never climbed—why would he?

*

I don't care, you're a writer,
you can say what you want,
but you got a lot of things wrong.

Dad never was gone for thirty minutes.
If he did get upset, he'd just go outside
and come back in.

And Jerusalem Hill isn't the name
of the mountain. It's the name
of the road behind the farm.

And he did so climb that mountain.
We climbed it a couple times.
We stopped going because

people started shooting guns up there.
It was a good place to make love.

Pinecroft Dairy

The family had sold the house
twenty years before
we parked in the gravel alongside

the small loop of road.
My uncle and I stood
in the unpaved driveway

and looked at the plain, white
two-story house where he had
essentially raised himself.

He pointed out where,
in the front yard, as a child,
he'd built his mini-golf course,

pressing tuna cans in the ground.
Afternoons, he'd play alone—
nine, eighteen, thirty-six holes.

Somewhere on the other side
of the loop, there had been
a path, and that path led

to a creek. Somewhere
in the past there was a culvert,
and atop it two boys pissing

on other boys as they walked through.
During high school, a neighbor
had let him use her phone

for the rare talk with a girl…
Pinecroft Dairy was a short drive—
in front of it, still,

the tree he used to climb.
We went there, each got a cone
and sat on one of the boulders

that bordered the parking lot,
my father's brother and me,
and the tumor growing

in his head, retracing
the footsteps of his childhood
while they were still visible

to him, while he
was still visible.
Pinecroft Dairy was no longer

Pinecroft Dairy, but it was
an ice cream place,
and the ice cream was good,

and right over there,
my uncle told me, he would
catch a bus to Worcester.

He had a membership
to the Y one summer,
and he'd shoot baskets,

but he was too shy
to ask to play in the games
with boys he didn't know.

Hardy's Heart

Hardy's heart was, upon his death,
removed from his body at his request.

The rest of him buried in Poet's Corner,
but his heart was buried with his first wife,

Emma, dead sixteen years.
Thick veined muscle, held in someone's hand,

stilled, purplish, a hint of damp.
Someone carried it to her grave,

someone planted the shovel and turned the earth,
someone smoothed the ground when it was done.

*

That's not quite true, a story I misheard.
Hardy wished to be buried next to Emma,

but the lords wanted him in Poet's Corner.
His second wife, Florence, was the one

who composed the compromise
to have his heart pulled from his chest—

which makes more sense. Who among us
would request that we divide our flesh

when we die? Well, as an organ donor,
I have, but that's a present to life,

not a doubling of death. Oh,
troublesome truth, that makes lyric

impossible to write, like Hardy's elegy
to Emma, when he imagines her

from beyond the grave casting a shadow
in the garden, though in his mind he knows

it can't be true. And yet, how he refuses
to turn around and confirm the truth—

That there was nothing in my belief—
the dead are in the ground. The verse he wrote,

though, shows he understood
that fancy, and verses, do little good.

*

The heart may have never made the trip.
Set on the kitchen table by the doctor,

and placed in a biscuit tin.
A rumor spread that the heart

was half-eaten by Hardy's cat.
Other rumors say the cat was killed

and buried with the heart's remains,
or that a pig's heart was used instead.

And—the internet dissolves all truth,
or hope for it—it was the local vicar

who wished to divide body and heart,
and Florence agreed only because

Westminster Abbey said the corpse
had to be cremated so as to "fit,"

and she did not want to burn his heart….
All this for something no longer alive.

All these words, too, for a guy whom
most accounts say became aloof and cruel,

gave Emma syphilis (another rumor),
and wouldn't tip his servants, even at Christmas.

Whitman

When he had finished writing, and crossing out
and standing and rewriting, and looking
out his window, and feeling the sun
so present with him as it shone through the glass
that it felt like a lover, when he saw the gulls
whirl and screech, and he sensed they were
talking in the language he understood if he just
sat and listened without judgment....
When
he finished, he walked out of his room,
down the curved wooden stairs and into the streets.
God, he loved the way his clothes
fell soft on his skin.

Me and Kenneth

Hearing Dean Young on a Poetry Foundation podcast talking of Kenneth
        Koch,
and reading his elegy for Koch,
and then, once I got to my office,
reading a few of Koch's poems in *Thank You,*
and then remembering Jeffrey Harrison's elegy for Koch that I read online,
and the AWP Panel that Mark Halliday was on commemorating Koch,

I think: I should write an elegy for Kenneth Koch!
I was in a class of his at Columbia. We read the anthology
of modern poetry he had put together with Kate Farrell,
Sleeping on the Wing. I probably wouldn't have been a poet
without that class and that book.

I wasn't a dedicated student then. When I went to my classes,
it was out of obligation. But Koch liked D.H. Lawrence so much,
and Apollinaire, and Mayakovsky, that I went to class
to hear him read their poems.

That was the year I started writing poems.
It was the year that I would walk five long blocks from my dorm
to my girlfriend's dorm, trying not to step on the cracks in the sidewalk,
seeing how many steps I could take without doing so, but not altering
my gait noticeably (I didn't want to look nuts).
Why didn't I look up, though? I was in New York City.
Numbers would always be there, and everywhere.
Irrelevant records would be set and broken and set,
and yet I counted. And when I made it to Nicole's door
(I changed her name),
I put the numbers aside and fell into her arms and her bed.
I wrote a sentimental love poem to her about those cracks, it even rhymed,
and when she read it she hugged me and kissed me and thanked me.

I don't know where that poem is now.
Nicole is a pediatrician in Rhode Island—I googled her a couple times.
I wonder if Kenneth Koch got to enjoy the word "googled."

And that was also the year that students put chains across the doors
of Hamilton Hall, where Koch's class was held, and if you wanted
to go to class, you had to take a tunnel from Philosophy Hall,
so even though I agreed with the protests—I wanted Columbia
to divest from South Africa—I would go to class. Sometimes.
I didn't go to class the day Koch read a few student poems.
I was telling another student how I had turned in my parody of
Lawrence's poem, "Snake"—God, that's a good poem.
You should read that after you finish reading this—and that student said,
"Oh, he read your poem in class!"

If I wanted to be maudlin I could make that moment
emblematic of my life:
how I missed the times when my words were read aloud,
and there may even be some truth to that. I'm a teacher
and students, if they talk about me at all, probably repeat things
I've said in class outside of class, among themselves,
so I don't get to hear my own words being appreciated.

If you're interested, there's more about me and Kenneth Koch
in my essay, "Me and Langston." But I didn't write about
the letter that he sent me a few months before he died,
after I'd written to him to thank him for *Sleeping on the Wing*
because I'd used the book in my creative writing classes
for a decade and I still loved it, even if my students didn't.
In the letter, he did what I did at the beginning of this stanza—
he told me about other books of his. "If you liked that book,
you might like…" he wrote.

Before I finish, I want to mention
that I was listening to the podcast about Kenneth Koch
on my ipod as I was walking to school on the day after Halloween.
Did Kenneth ever hear that word, "ipod"?
And as I was walking, and listening to him read a poem,
and then Dean Young read his elegy on the podcast through a cell phone—
"Elegy on a Toy Piano," it's called—
I was seeing how many steps I could take, consecutively,
without stepping on a crack.

Bicycle

Only you make the city feel
both small and large.
With each push, legs pulsing
circular, I hear wind
speaking of what's left behind.

There are rules only I
can break, half-pedestrian,
half-vehicle—the envy
of those plodding on foot,
those convulsed in traffic.

Sometimes I sing for joy,
sometimes to rub it in.

*

You move me, and though my body
breathes and churns it is your pace
I live by. Like a fish
you dart and angle. I ride your spine,
my head over yours, your body
spinning beneath me,
pushing the ground behind us.

My feet almost touch the earth,
my body nearly flies.

*

I squeeze you
to make you
stop moving
me

*

Talk to me about the rust
speckling your frame.
You must have heard my cartilage
crack with every pedal push.
How does one live tarnished
and corroded?

Aging is just the way
we take in water, the effects
of oxygen, the movement
of electrons. We aren't only
the iron of the present,
we are what gets left behind
in every interaction.

*

At night, in the shed's darkness
your dreams unspool: mountain switchbacks,
dirt trails, ramps and leaps, the healthy shudder
of landing, or a nice long greasing,
your chain guided through oily palms.
Upright, a lock binding wheel to frame,
a hairy shifting beneath you—rat, skunk—
some beast who knows you're more animal
than gear, that sniffs your travels in your treads
and pisses in the corner,

the scent like music to you, a melody
layered into the shades of night, dissipating
into dawn's sudden mist.

After Tu Fu

Night Drive

The headlights gather at the tollbooth like a flock of stars.
The toll-taker sits in her box, speaking only numbers.

Once freed, the cars find their own rhythm in the night,
while above, the moon arches an eyebrow.

What does it mean, this motion?
My knees ache too much for these long drives.

A mother skunk runs from the turnpike,
her young one dead on the road.

Leaving My Parents' Cottage

The sunset and its orange clouds have gone.
The mosquitoes, who came with the dusk,

gone, too, into the chill dark.
Beyond the porchlight's reach, the ocean

collides with the rocks, eternal sound.
We back out of the driveway,

Gravel scraping as if to clutch us here,
roll down the windows and let in the night.

My parents dance in our headlights,
their parting gift.

To My Son

You ask why we live
in a small, messy house full of books.

And I ask: a pool table?
A bathroom so large? For what?

My soul has never loved our two-bit lives,
but it has no gaudy desires, either.

There's a hammock in our backyard.
We can eat on the porch if we wish.

Between Men and Women

What is it between men and women?
For thousands of years, more pain than joy.

In marriages—some love, much sorrow.
Oh, such work to keep each other happy!

But it can be honest work, like tending a garden,
or building a shed, or writing.

Summer Night

The hostas have been cut,
stems in a bag on our porch,

like people standing in a crowded room.
I turned the pile of dead leaves today,

and beetles danced in the wet loam.
What is this myth called freedom?

In the backyard's evening sky,
trees play catch with a swallow.

Thoughts of Tu Fu

When I feel lonely, I should think of Tu Fu.
Exiled, family and friends
hundreds of miles downriver.

His wine a thin blanket,
his eyes too dull to read,
talking to the moon.

II.
(Monologues)

Prayer to My People

Don't you know that love is holy
Can't you see that I am only
All the things you've told to me

And when I ask to be forgiven
For the ways I've failed at living
Will you sing a song to me

Territory

Sometimes, even I don't believe my life,
the one I shared with Carl tonight

before I danced. I suck at dancing.
I came to it late. Still, people watch me,

fascinated. When I turn, slowly, counting
the beats in my head, I feel their eyes.

Carl saw this, saw how the other students
would follow me in the mirror,

trusting that I remembered the steps,
even when I had no idea.

"You should take more dance classes,"
he said to me one day. I thought

he was hitting on me, which was O.K.,
though I wasn't really interested.

He had a bald patch on the back
of his head, his breath was stale coffee.

It's funny, how it turned out he was straight,
and how I took five of his classes,

and it was funny how I ended up
eating a bagel with him in Cambridge

before the collegiate dance festival,
students crowding tables around us.

Every time someone opened the door
spring blew through the place.

Carl was more nervous than I was.
"You ready?" he said a few times,

then, "You'll do great." Truth is
I just didn't care. I wanted to do well

for Carl, but really, none of the students there
were that good, otherwise they'd be in

a conservatory somewhere. It wasn't like
I was dreaming of a career as a dancer.

It was something I liked to do and
people liked to watch me.

*

I was thinking about the sting of Gabe's stubble
when I walked into the kitchen's harsh light.

Mom was there, in a Christmasy sweater,
green and red and white with blocky reindeer,

and before I said anything, she said—
I'll never forget this—"I'm going to ask

you one question and I want the truth.
Are you gay?" I looked at her and thought,

here it goes, and said "Yes,"
and she threw the toaster at me,

and then dishes, mugs,
anything she could pull from the cupboards….

The cops said I should get some of my stuff
and leave. It still kills me that I couldn't take

my aquarium ("Long gone," she said a week later
during our last phone call). The bruise on my cheek

wasn't serious enough to press charges.
I didn't want to press charges anyway, that night,

though, looking back, I kind of wish I had.
"Do you have someplace to go?" one cop asked

as I stood on the lawn. I could see my mother
through the front window, calmly talking

to another cop. "Bitch!" I screamed, and the cop
with me put one hand on my chest, the other

on my shoulder. "That's not gonna help things,"
he said, "Do you have someplace you can go?"

I looked at him. I could feel his palm pressed
against me. His eyes gave me no sympathy,

but no hate. He'd seen this shit before.
He drove me to Gabe's place and took

my two duffle bags out of the trunk, set them
on the pavement like a taxi driver and said "O.K.,"

and I was standing deep in the Lowell night,
shivering outside Gabe's beat-up apartment.

My folded paycheck from CVS in my jeans pocket,
the only money I had. I was sixteen.

*

The spring after my mom threw me out
Gabe graduated and we moved in with his sister,

an apartment in South Boston. Gabe started
looking for work, and I wanted to do that, too,

but he said, "Jared, if you don't get your diploma now,
you'll be fucked for your whole life,"

so I spent a week going into South Boston High
and telling my story to different people.

There was this one guidance counselor—she
was wearing jeans, I remember, because

that seemed too casual—and after she heard me
she said, "You've got a year. Let's get you through."

I wanted to hug her then. Instead, I nodded.
I couldn't speak. And when I walked out of the school

I ran into a McDonalds bathroom, locked myself
in a stall, and sobbed. I was sitting on the toilet lid;

the flimsy plastic felt like it might crack.
It was there that I really said goodbye

to my mother, that I just didn't care anymore
what she had said, all the "faggots" she spit at me.

"Let's get you through," rinsed off the venom.
Someone opened the bathroom door.

I flushed the toilet to drown my sniffles
and stood. There, on the stall wall,

someone had scraped, "Fags Die." Honestly,
I laughed—to see that message *then.*

I took out my apartment key and scratched
a "t" after "Die"—"Fags Diet." I don't know

what I meant by it, but it felt good
cutting through the paint and metal.

*

Carl was more stunned than I thought he'd be
when I told him about Henry and our year

in Capilla. He couldn't believe that I was accepted
by Henry's family, how they let us sleep together,

sharing a room with his young brother and sister,
or how a little village in the Dominican

didn't care that one of their own brought home
a gringo pájaro. I was too young to know

how unreal it all was. I was just happy to be
in a house where people didn't hate me.

Everyone in Capilla was related to Henry.
He was the only gay man there, but Henry

told me that an uncle of his who lived
in Santa Domingo was gay, too, and he came back

to the village on Christmas and other holidays
with gifts for the children. I don't remember

Henry much in that house. I remember when
we met at the MFA Boston, how he seemed

so at ease talking to me, a stranger, and how
the sex wasn't rough, or steamy,

just an extension of our friendship,
what one did after sharing a bottle of wine.

I think it's why, in the end, I left him.

*

I didn't tell Carl this, but when I think
of those two years in Capilla, I think more

of Henry's brother and sister than of him,
how they ran—their spindly brown bodies,

the way they would laugh at my Spanish.
I remember some local church had been given

a pile of children's books, in English,
and they would bring a handful to me,

grab my hand and pull me to one of the mattresses
in the room where we slept. We'd flop down

and I would read, taking on different voices
for the characters. They only half-understood,

but they loved it—and I loved it, a way to pass
the slow days. I loved Tito and Mina nestled

on either side of me, the rich smell of their
sweaty hair, a hand moving up and down

my arm absentmindedly. And when they'd play
I'd hear them repeat phrases from the books.

For a month, all the village kids were quacking
and saying, "Make way for ducklings."

*

Homeless. I never thought of the word
that summer I would sleep in the park

near Harvard. Gabe had found someone else,
and one day I just loaded up a duffle bag,

grabbed a couple oranges and bagels
and left. I haven't seen him since.

Homeless. I never thought of it in Buenos Aires,
Austin, L.A., Newark—all those cities

after Capilla where I hustled myself
for a bed, a room, food. Some stories

I won't tell, even now. The shade
of the overpass, the raid on the shelter,

the men with broken teeth, the blood
on the blade, drops crusting the dirt.

When the word came up in Sociology
this year, I mentioned that I'd been homeless,

and the professor treated me like I was
an expert. I told her I didn't know

much, had never studied it….
She just wanted to hear my stories.

I started to share one, and the other students
looked at me like I was on a reality show.

Who needs that? "You don't want to know," I said.
I couldn't explain it then, but now I get it:

I'm in school to find out what happened to me.

*

Last year, when I was into painting, I tried oils—
tried to paint that hotel room in North Jersey

where I blew guys for 30 bucks, but I couldn't
get it right. I probably just wasn't good enough,

but there seemed no way to get into the painting
how dark and ugly that room felt to me, how,

even though it reeked of disinfectant,
I could only see it as if in a dream, stinking

with the rankness of crotch sweat, of assholes,
full of shadows and the colors of hurt—brown, deep blue,

maroon. When I tried to paint it that way, it just didn't
feel honest. I knew I was putting in too many

of my own feelings; it dripped melodrama....
The room itself was so nondescript.

Nothing wrong with it, too bland to be tacky.
I tried to paint it that way, too, but that felt wrong.

The dark print curtains, the polyester bedspread.
It all seemed too quaintly American: calm,

bare. I even tried to include the expensive watch
one of the johns took off and left on the nightstand—

I had considered trying to steal it. Maybe I should
have just put two people in the painting, the server

and the served. Screw surrealism, screw subtlety.
Screw distance. Maybe I should have put a man

sitting on a bed with his pants down and me
between his legs, on my knees, maybe I should have painted

just my bent, bony knees on that itchy carpet.

*

When the music began, I leapt and crashed
to the floor, trying to make as much noise

as possible. And then I gradually worked myself
upright, swerving my shoulders, rolling

and stretching my neck like some animal.
People looked at my face, and I stared back,

trying to get the feel and shape and tone
of that cop's face on the front lawn

so many years ago. I gave nothing away.
I thrashed a little—I've done so much fucking

I know how to thrash—and then I slowed
it all down, easing into stillness. I could've

done anything at that moment, screamed,
scratched my armpit, or even started tap dancing.

I could've just stopped and walked offstage
as if I had a call to make. I liked that.

I liked that I had reached a point
where all there was

was freedom.

*

Sometimes I joke and call Jeffrey my Sugar Daddy.
Of course, he is. I was sharing an apartment

with three women, going to school, and working
full-time at Stop & Shop when we met.

Now I'm in a house, a fucking house!
He's thirty, five years older than me.

I don't get his job—selling pharmaceuticals—
but it pays a lot better than mine.

We've been together almost two years.
I haven't really gotten monogamy either.

After all those johns, it just seems like a con,
but Jeffrey and I talk about it—a lot.

He wanted to give me flowers after the dance.
I told him if he tried, we were over.

We were both probably joking.
We hung around the reception, and a few

queers told me how fab I was,
and, of course, the women in their spandex

from the other schools couldn't stop gushing about me.
Carl, I could tell, was proud of me, and proud

of himself, for having picked me,
for having noticed my talent and supported me.

I sound like I'm ungrateful, but I'm not.
It was all good. And when it was over,

Jeffrey, Carl and I walked through the chill
April night back to Jeff's car. Carl had asked

for a ride to South Station. The city, beyond
the closed windows, felt silent, full of lights

and shadows, and I couldn't help but notice
the haunts, the corners, the sidewalks that I knew

from that time after high school and before
the Dominican. Jeffrey and Carl were making

awkward small talk.... How calm the world.
How calm *my* world. I fingered the pack

of cigarettes in my jacket pocket, anxious
to light one up once we'd dropped Carl off.

*

Jeffrey gave me a fishtank for my birthday
two months after I moved in. Twenty gallons.

and a gift card to buy fish and fake plants.
I'd had that tank when I was growing up,

and he knew I loved to go to the Aquarium.
I got it running, picked out a three-inch tigershark

and some fish big and tough enough so that
the shark wouldn't eat them. I spent too much

on this huge sunken ship to ornament
the tank. I liked the broken mast

and missing planks, hints of tragedy.
When I put the fish in, two died right away,

and the others were always nipping each other.
This one guppy, all orange and blue

with streaming fins, got it the worst,
and didn't last, swimming in a sad, irregular circle,

then upside down, then death. Jeffrey would
come home from work and I'd be there,

sitting in the armchair, watching the remaining fish
come to know each other, their aggression easing

into acceptance, their territory understood.

Indiana

Just last month I looked at Martin and I knew,
suddenly, that I was content, and a wave

washed through me, and I could almost see
all the flotsam and debris of my life

ebbing, dispersing in April's air,
and if I believed in some higher power,

I would say I felt it at that moment.
Martin wasn't smiling at me, or giggling

like he does when he's slapping water
out of the tub. He was just sitting

on our front porch watching a few ants,
his brown hair curled around his ears.

*

Indiana. The mild, wooded hills
and the bustle of students:

backpacks and bicycles and
the sour beer smell of the bars,

and where, in time, I met Cal
and my life. Who would've thought?

I wanted to go back east as soon
as I moved out here. I knew

Henry and I were doomed
even before I said I'd join him.

Henry made me laugh. I bet he could
still make me laugh, but he drank

and lied about being vegetarian.
How weird to see him downtown

sitting in Josie's Pub, eating
a barbecue chicken sandwich,

the glob of sauce on the edge
of his mouth. I was stunned.

I walked right over to him,
"What are you doing?" And he

looked at me, then at the two guys
he was with—coworkers—

and they all smiled. It was a joke to him.
I had moved 800 miles for a joke.

*

Let me say it: my father molested me.
My family—mother, sisters—

are split over who to believe.
It crushed me for years, a secret

I only alluded to with friends,
wrote about elliptically in poems

and essays. It was behind every
bitchy conversation with my mother

about why, if I was so smart,
I kept dropping out of college.

It was there, always,
scattered through my days

and my words like shards
from a broken mirror, but

I just couldn't say it.

*

I used to believe that I'd be killed
by a man. I dated them,

even lived with them, but I sensed
there was something deep inside them

that kept us separate, and that
at some moment, this thing would surface,

smoking, and it would clutch me
by the throat and would not let go

and I would turn my eyes to him—
to it—and it would not have eyes,

or rather, its eyes were turned inward
and I could only see the nexus

of veins and nerves that pulsed
and shimmied as my windpipe gave in

and the last voice in my head
would be my own saying

You always knew this would happen,
and still—still!—you let it happen.

*

If it wasn't for that job in the library
I'd have left Bloomington.

Cal worked the stacks, supervising
the work-studies who put away the books.

In the caf, at lunch, all us staff
would sit and joke about the students—

like the one looking for "that book
that says God is dead. I think it's green."

One lunch, after the rest of the crew had left,
and I was sitting across from Cal

eating grapes—green grapes—he said
"Do you know that I like you?"

and I almost choked. Even now,
five years later, whenever we have grapes,

we share a look, and the first time
I diced grapes for Martin

and set them on his tray,
and he fisted them and pushed them

into his mouth and then
wriggled enthusiastically

in his high chair, as if dancing…
yeah, I cried.

*

Senior year of high school I tried to tell.
My parents had been divorced for years.

My mother wouldn't look at me.
She spoke to me like I was eight

and making up a story. The honey
in her voice sickened me

bringing me back to when
I *was* eight…those baths…

When my father stopped by that Christmas
I felt my family eying me,

and I let him hug me, kiss my cheek.
I even hugged him back. I could tell

my mother and Marie, my oldest sister,
were satisfied. They thought that was

the end of it. It was the end
of something. I moved out

after graduation that spring
and never touched my father again.

*

I remember every paper I didn't finish
and why. There isn't one of them

I didn't start. I'd get a few pages down
and then something happened.

I'd read over my words, and it all
seemed obvious—of course James Baldwin

was saying that love was difficult. Worse,
my words seemed incoherent. First,

I couldn't follow my thoughts
from one sentence to the next,

and then even the sentences themselves
broke down, the gaps between words too big

for the words to connect, and I couldn't believe
there'd been a time when what I wrote,

when what I thought, made sense to me.

*

Indiana spreads out. When I take Martin
to the backyard, I worry he will

just run and run, until he reaches
the cornfields beyond the highway

and—crinkle, swish—disappears.
The towns, even Bloomington,

seem like desperate attempts
to gather against the emptiness. It's all

so different than Boston, where everything
presses you in—where there's the ocean,

that final cold barrier. Some days
I couldn't even look at it. And the smell!

Those mornings when the fog rolled in,
it flooded my pores, as present

as memory, reminding me where I was,
its scent thick with the message

that I wasn't going anywhere….

*

I don't understand men, even Cal,
how he can watch poker on TV,

or like motorcycles and their whiff
of death. But I love him, I really do,

and if I could put down how
tender he is, I would, but I don't

understand it—maybe that's
one more essay I'll never finish.

I can live with that. Some sunny days
when Martin's napping, I carry

myself and a book out to the backyard
and lie in the long, young spring grass

(Spring comes so early here!)
and close my eyes, and stretch my arms

as if to let the whole world in,
as if to embrace the air. A hint of breeze.

The sun coats my skin, and the grass blades
trembling in the wind seem to be touching me,

and it feels good.

Cirinna

When Cirinna died, I was only 15.
Now I'm twice that, but the image

of her opened wrists over the tub's edge,
the dried blood streaking the white enamel,

is tattooed on my life. I inked it
& I have refused to let it fade.

Even if I wanted to I'm afraid
to let it go. It's the source of my writing

& art. That image of her? It's imagined.
I never saw her slumped on the tile floor,

but I have drawn it, & written it,
dreamed it, & yes, lived it.

*

"Don't just grab my ass. You want it,
you ask me for it. Be a man,

not a shit!" When Cirinna said that
to the jock in the hallway

I fell in love, & when he said,
smirking, "Alright, you and me,"

& tilted his chin, she scanned his body,
letting the crowd gather, & said,

"Fuck, no!" She knew what she wanted.
At fifteen, she knew what she wanted.

*

The FotoMat drove me to coke:
eight hour shifts in that closet

in the mall parking lot, shelves
full of other people's lives

waiting to be picked up
through the tiny window.

I fucked there & never ate.
The fucking was out of boredom

& for the thrill, the risk.
The fasting was serious. I'd be

so dizzy with hunger the last hours
I'd put up the "Back in 5 minutes" sign

& slump to the floor.
I'd try to read, but the letters blurred

& shimmered & taunted me
& so even though Michelle Tea

& Plath saved my life back then,
I couldn't get through a page,

a poem, & I'd just wait,
my mind floating through images

& aches, the occasional honk
from a frustrated customer

like someone moving furniture
in a nearby universe.

Who wouldn't start snorting coke?

*

College was better than work,
but it was boring, too. Those teachers

who tried to get everyone talking—
forced blabber until they all

collected their participation points.
I know I drove my profs crazy

by skipping half the classes, but I was
either purging, or coming off a coke high,

or thinking about my life, & Cirinna,
& just too miserable

to look at another human being….
I thought I was going to be an artist,

carried a sketchbook all the time.
Nearly all my drawings were of her.

I didn't want to forget a feature.
I'd draw her in a coffin, with open eyes,

or in a white dress in the recesses
of a cemetery, full moon stretching

the shadows of gravestones.
When I showed them to my drawing prof,

he flipped through them in less
than a minute, grimaced, shrugged.

I remember just one word: "juvenile."

*

The year I dropped out, there were two men.
The one who beat me, & Josh, the one

who got me pregnant. All the sad shit
intensified with them: the cutting,

the drinking, dropping to 80 pounds.
I won't talk about the beatings

won't even say the fucker's name,
but Josh & I had something.

I used to think he kept me high
because he loved me, & when he'd come home

& line the coke, & give me almost half
I'd be so grateful, I'd blow him

& then we'd go to Taco Bell
& order four tacos each

& I'd puke mine out in the store's bathroom,
the yellow bucket & mop in the corner,

then come back & listen to him
tell me I needed to get my shit together.

*

I was so fucked up those years,
so consumed with death

& so ignorant, so obsessed
with the black clothes & boots,

so bruised from beatings & harangues,
that I almost fell in love with hate.

I still remember adding a small swastika
in the corner of one of my sketches

of Cirinna. All that day, driving through town
or in his apartment, I kept seeing its shape:

in the sharp bend of a tree limb,
in the floor tiles & door frames.

I saw it more than I saw her,
so I knew it was wrong,

& that night I took my sketchbook
into the bathroom, & rubbed the eraser

into the swastika, but I couldn't make it
disappear completely, so I drew

a lily over it, a dying lily.

*

I don't have a story for you about how I escaped
(Have I escaped?). I'd swear off booze

& drugs every few months, & though
I'd relapse, it became easier & easier

to say no. The same with men.
The miscarriage shook me—I hadn't known

I'd be so relieved…& so sad.
& then my parents let me move back

with them when my father got sick.
& then, & then, & then…

& suddenly I was pregnant again,
& there was Liam, & his dad

agreed to help raise him, & I felt
so adult. Through it all, Cirinna

was the one constant—the raspberry smell
from her room, her cracked leather jacket

folded in the box I kept under my bed.
I held onto her, & we promised each other

things I can't tell you, even now.

*

No, we never had sex.
No, we never cut ourselves

& rubbed our blood together—
I wish we had. We wore black,

thickened our eyes with mascara.
& sealed our mouths with black lipstick.

We'd hang out in her room & listen
to bands I still listen to today,

though now it's for nostalgia—
they're not that good. We'd shoplift, get high.

We'd hang out in the woods & cry.
The fire in the school's equipment shed?

That was us the week before....
I only knew her nine months.

I still don't know why.

*

Every so often, I'll look in the mirror
and think *I should be dead by now.*

It doesn't make me thankful,
it makes me angry: why am I still here?

All the clichés—my son, my parents,
poetry—bore me. I feel I was born

to suffer, to vomit up what
I take in—food, drugs, words.

Some nights I lie in bed & feel Sylvia
lying next to me, at my back,

her arms folded against her small chest,
just touching my spine.

It's so real it's real. I close
my eyes. She's weeping,

& then she begins to talk,
to recite a poem in some lost

guttural tongue. God, I know
it's not real, even when I turn,

& see her bottomless eyes, & touch—
yes touch!—her cheek & it feels

warmer, & more damp, than my own,
more filled with the fuse of life

& I wonder if I'm something
she imagined…

had I let her create me?
I leap out of bed & go to the kitchen

& flick on the light, the rest of the house
swaddled in darkness, & I write:

I write angry poems about what he
did to me, I write elegies to the child

I didn't have. I write unforgiving poems
& unforgivable poems,

rants that expose my selfishness,
my ego, my absurd obsession

with a teenager who died
more than a decade ago. *Cirinna…*

I should be dead by now.

*

My friend Ray called me, affectionately,
histrionic. "I guess so," I said, but

I don't like that word, it suggests
I'm not being authentic, & my most

authentic self is this frazzled, electric
heartbeat. I'm proud of how

I kicked bulimia, how I salvaged Cirinna
In my poems, & myself….

The past. My past. It would torture me
if I let it. When I returned to school

two years ago, I had to write a letter
explaining why I should be readmitted

after so many failed classes. I wrote
the whole story, & when I met

with some committee, they seemed just a bit
more scared of saying no than saying yes,

& so, last spring, after ten years,
I finished. I stood outside

among the folding chairs, families
snapping pictures, black robes,

clutched my diploma & ate
the chocolate-covered strawberries

as Liam smeared his across his face
and leaned against my leg. My robe,

so loose & bulky, made me feel
as if I didn't have a body.

My legs & arms had disappeared—
& my tattoos & scars? Gone.

*

You might think I'm a horrible mother
with my binges & moods

& wonder about my five year old.
Well, fuck you. But know, too,

that my parents live a few blocks away,
know that I do the birthday parties

& Halloween, that I watch videos
with Liam. Know that he loves me.

"I want to be King of Lynn,"
he said last week….

Last summer, when we went to Six Flags
I took him on the Scrambler.

He was gnawing on his sweatshirt
as the cars clinked up the incline.

Just as we crested I heard the guy
behind me say to the girl with him

"Hold on," & then his voice got cruel,
"Hold on, you cunt." Say what you want

about me, but know that I left that life.
I killed it. Don't tell me it was easy.

*

Cirinna, there are times now
I want you to leave me alone,

but I've used so many words
to make you, that you're more solid

than Liam, & I feel I'm back
to those morbid clichés I drew

years ago. You appear to me
bleeding, eyes wider than they ever were

in life, & I caress your face
& my hand sinks into your flesh

& I'm both fascinated &
a little bored & I'd like you

to climb down off my dresser
& squeeze into the crack

in the floorboard, so that
every so often as I cross the room

& hear a squeak, I'll say
"There's Cirinna," & smile

& I won't feel guilt when I live
a day, a week, a month

without a thought of you.

III.

Blueberries

On the northern tip of Cape Ann,
on the ridge overlooking the quarry,
just off the wide gravel path
that leads to Halibut Point:

blueberries. Some dusky grey,
some so deep blue
they are almost purple,
almost black, small blueberries,

pert, dark pearls hanging among
unripe green pebbles.
These berries grew on this ridge
before Puritans, Pilgrims, Christians.

They lived their quick lives and deaths
with the blackbirds and cormorants.
Were they thicker then? Less
mercury in their roots? Were they

the same deep, dusky shades
that cover the hillside now,
raindrops of the night that approaches
across the unruly Atlantic?

Somewhere beyond the brush
and trees, the flat water
of the abandoned quarry
is swallowing the evening sky.

Father Bob

It was the night we were told we couldn't pretend we were Catholic.
The priest turned only toward you and said, "It's between you and God."
And you cried.

I hope we didn't shake his hand before we walked into the night snow
for the long walk to our apartment where we had a dresser in the closet
and a computer heavy as death.

The flakes surrounded us; the wind scraped our cheeks. We were almost lost.
Snow, wind, block after block, past a sheet hanging from a dorm's window
with black words: FUCK IRAQ.

We hoped the sweet shop was open, so we could buy peanut butter balls,
and then we overheard "Bush bombing Baghdad."
The war had begun.

Your scarf so red it seemed alive, your thrift store black coat darker
than the purple night. The snow deepening, thickening.
The sweet shop was closed.

A car, and another, swerved its headlights across the long white field
where, soon, a tent city of protest would arise,
mud and Frisbees.

Can you see our little house? Its olive green
showing in the streetlight as we came up the alley to the back steps
and unlocked the door—

into the tiny kitchen that we could hardly fit in together.
Taking our shoes off, slush ribbing the floor. It wasn't late,
but it felt late.

It felt like the only thing to do was lie on the futon, under the covers,
and listen to the radio, to words we didn't want to hear, falling.
Our country less our country, and more our country.

The Diseased Tree

The word *Lebanon* in the air over breakfast,
spoken by the radio, as, seated at the bottom of our staircase,
my love and our two sons watch workers
dismantle the diseased tree. "It deserves an audience.
The end of such an impressive life...." And a limb
knocks down but does not snap the cable line,
and Guthrie, in only his underwear, spills Eileen's iced tea,
and Aidan laces his sneakers for basketball camp,
while I line up my work for the day, sitting on the toilet.

Nothing is fair. Not the life I wished to have led,
with me better at everything, and more loved,
not the way the day is too hot, or too cloudy,
or how, in its perfection, it reminds us
how few perfect days there are. Even a string
of perfect days—can you believe this weather?
80 degrees, no humidity, a casual cloud drifting by
like an appreciative, undiscerning audience—
even such a string reminds me of the week in September
when the towers melted. God, the breath of fall
in those days. To get away from the news,
we drove to pick apples, and all along
the main street of Peabody were people, standing,
or in lawn chairs holding—not waving—American flags.
Plaintive, and curled in upon themselves,
like human question marks. It went on
for over a mile, past the red cross tent,
past Bunghole Liquors. Like every other food
those first weeks after, the apples had no taste.
Tart, sweet, crisp, juicy, whatever.

"Did you see that? It knocked a chunk out of the trunk!"
Oh, Guthrie, my youngest and most fierce—
"Why do they have to have a war? Why don't they just vote?"
you asked, and you studied the Civil War last year, asking me
to read you a turgid biography of Lee,
watching Ken Burns' documentary
until, halfway through, you said you'd had enough—
it was giving you bad dreams. And your occasional
bedtime sobs about mortality; you couldn't accept
my Whitmanic explanation—just last night
you wanted to calculate how many minutes
you had left to live. And now your joy
at the force with which the descending branch
struck the trunk, the flurry of sawdust—a dusting
of August snow.

Salem Common On Training Day

—a painting by George Ropes Jr., 1808

The elm trees rise up like flames.
They line the common,
dwarfing the regiments and
their puny flags—red and white.

The soldiers are too far away
to see clearly—some red blurs,
some blue. Phalanxes.
No one is watching. The families

and children and wagons
and horses in the foreground
seem to pass slowly in front
of the elms. In the middle distance,

shadowy, a brown mass
of citizens surrounds
some political speaker.
Everyone, save

the strolling civilians
and their leaping dogs,
is inside the white fence
that borders the common.

The republic is thirty-two years old.
No planes, of course, in the sky, just
specks of gulls, and dirty
cotton ball clouds. The elms,

not yet destroyed by disease,
seem like they are trying to hold
back the sunset, which explodes
orange at the tips of their leaves.

Scene From Abu Ghraib

Two American
soldiers

scoop a dead
Iraqi's

brains from his
skull

while another takes
photos.

Birds in Their Habitats

There's a video going around Facebook of an eagle
that swoops down to clutch a toddler in a park,
then lifts, the child rising with it a few feet
before slipping from its grasp and thudding to earth.
Like so much we see, it was all fake.

I wonder if the two-year-old was really crying
at the end of the clip, or if that, too, was phony.
It sounded like real crying. It sounded almost as real
as the threatening squawk of that seagull
guarding those broken shells and their gobbets.

In a chapter of *The Hobbit,* "Out Of the Frying Pan,
Into the Fire," Bilbo and the dwarves are trapped
in trees, and goblins light fires below them.
Then, eagles pluck them out of the smoky leaves.
That sounds fake, too, doesn't it? Or at least really lucky.

What was that eagle doing, trying to snatch that toddler?
Yes, it's a bird of prey, it was probably hungry,
but what if it knew what we did to each other?
What if it was simply saying *Enough?*
I don't know what to believe anymore.

On Mount Sinjar, thousands are trapped, starving.
If they're lucky, they may see a rare bearded vulture.
Down the beach, a few cormorants raise their crooked wings.
How threatening they look, though they don't know it.
They're just drying their feathers in the sun.

Nation Building

Some days, when I'm bored with TV,
I begin to build a nation. Always begin.
I gather a slave or two, suggest they start
piling blocks of marble, even, if I have time,
show them a picture of The Capitol, or whatever
monument I've been dreaming. And while I leave
them to do this work "if they get around to it,"
I might sit down and start drafting documents
anticipating my nation's archives. Or I might
compose folk songs, anticipating folk.
Always, in the words, or notes, is the sludge
of my world. There's the damp cardboard
in the blue plastic recycling bin
on the sidewalk. There's the question:
how to build a nation and still have friends?
And then I need to check the weather,
clean the fish tank. I can actually feel
the leaking in the attic. I put Stevie Wonder
on the turntable and, if anyone is around,
they laugh. I talk about a design for a flag
with someone who pays to listen to me,
and then, driving out of my hometown,
a few inches of snow on the fields and forests:
a dead deer curled on the road's shoulder,
and, a few minutes later, the silhouette
of a live deer leaping across the road
fifty yards ahead. See? The nation never
gets finished. There's never even enough
for a good ruin. I voted last fall,
and it might have been counted. When
I was in ninth grade and my class stood
to recite the pledge of allegiance, I stood,

but I did not speak the words, dropped
a hand into my pocket and fingered the nickels
I would gamble on the bus ride home.

In the Months of the Roaches

I tried to love you
as you appeared:
efficient, eager,
gathering at the least crumb.
A drop of orange juice meant
Party! The fear of you
crawling into my month-old
son's ear never did fade,
though, and when I witnessed
your hatching upon
the shower curtain—
a hundred white dots
scrambling—I didn't
celebrate your sheer joy
at life: The fresh dampness
of waking in a bathroom
four feet from the floor,
a nude man grimacing at you.
How wonderful, you thought,
heading for the drain,
How much we have
to live for.

The Sofa

I do not love words, but I consider them friends.
They cannot always be trusted, but neither can I.
When they come to me in the night,
I toss off the covers and leave my wife sleeping.

It is always a little cold those nights,
and when our conversation pauses,
words and I both listen for what may have been
a mouse.
            If I trusted words more, would I
love my family less? If I could
never trust words, I would learn to kill.

I sip some water from a blue plastic cup
and lean back on our yard-sale sofa
that our sons have pocked with holes,
jabbing pens through the cushions.

Out the window, the first tints of light—

Salem, Mass

I hope I never forget that pack of middle-schoolers
at the playground near my house, how they acted
like middle-schoolers, shouting their conversations
across the neighborhood as if showing off new sneakers,
the boys doing mean things to the girls,
the girls saying mean things about each other.
If I hadn't been at the jungle gym with my two-year-old,
I'm sure they would have been smashing bottles
on the basketball court.

Then, like pigeons when popcorn spills,
they flocked to a spot under the basket.
Some squealed. A boy held out his arm,
keeping others back. "It's alive," I heard one say,
and suddenly one boy was cupping a baby bird
in his hand as another climbed the pole
that held up the net. "Give it to me,"
said the boy on the pole, and he took the bird
and placed it in the nest that was behind the backboard.

Too much misery goes down
in this city I call my home. I'm in no mood
to list it here, now. In my children's schools,
the schools where my wife teaches,
it's all too clear which kids won't get past
their dead mother, their addicted father, the fact
that no one has ever read them a book....

It was just one small bird
who must have had a stupid parent—
who would build a nest
on the backside of a backboard?—

but that afternoon it was safe,
and as I chased my son, trying to stop him
from stepping in the dog shit,
the voices of the middle-schoolers fading
as they made their way up the block
to go play video games and pretend to kill things,
as I held his hand while he zipped down the slide
I thought, yeah, I guess I could live here
for the rest of my life.

Yellow Leaves on a Blue Plastic Slide

Which is more colorful,
death or childhood?
Or is it their juxtaposition
that gives each its shine?

Just beyond this playground
runs the train, then the river.
One empties into the city,
the other, the sea.

Laid-Off Elementary School Librarian

When the new principal
under the direction
of the educational
consulting company
asks you to train
your minimum-wage replacement
and the local papers
praise all the "reforms"
and even your friends
move to the suburbs and believe
the brown skin of the children you teach
must be avoided,
when your Saturdays
buying used books for those children
and the darkening afternoons
putting those books away
so they can check them out again
seem a lost, wasted life,
remember your walk
to and from school
through the downtown
that's still your downtown
and the way your students
wrap their arms around your leg
when they see you on the street
and how the older ones
from years before—
even, sometimes, the boys—
hug you in Market Basket
or at the Halloween Parade
and pronounce your name
wrong, like they used to,

Mizgerald, Mizgerald!
and then tell you
what books they've been reading.

The Vow

for E.F.

"Life's too short not to jump in the ocean every day,"
said an old man one afternoon, scooping the Atlantic
and slapping it across his chest, and so
we have tried to jump in the ocean every day—
well, every day in summer.

It's only a ten-minute ride from our house—
a small, tame, nearly empty beach
—and we drop our bodies into the brine,
wiggling our limbs in a slow dance.
We talk about her work, mine,
review our children, nearly adults, note
a backlit cloud, some local news,
and gossip, always a dab of gossip.

Above us, the late day sky spreads
pink and rose over the sailboats,
the old arcade, the bridge that spans
the river's mouth. On the slime-coated rocks,
a young girl and boy clamber for hermit crabs,
collect them in a green pail.
Their mother sits on a towel, gazing past us.

When they shift the pail, I hear the splash and rattle
all the way from here, where we dog paddle,
keeping our promise to ourselves
in the meager waves, out just over our heads.

The Stream

The Irish folk singer's voice spills from the radio.
She sees her lover under a tree, and I,
rinsing dishes at the kitchen sink, the glow
of the neighbors' porch light beyond the window,
see the green bank of the stream that, like a wound,
cut through the campus, and the huge tree on that bank.

Whatever grew from that day, gnarled and sturdy,
brown and flowering, branches snapping in the wind,
is not the creature of that day, green and undulating,
sinuous as a snake, and as wondrous,
some visitor from a world without time.

She is its center, reading beneath that tree,
looking up at me on the path with the students
marching class to class, the circle of rooms
that made our lives, looking up and smiling.

The song aches with young love.
I brush rice off the plates, blind in the glow
of that decades-gone day, the violent sweet green
of the leaves and grass, the shudder of spring,
the brown rugged bark, the open book, the babble
of students in a time before headphones,

and her beneath the tree, knees emerging
from shorts into the spring sun that coats everything,
even the shade, all so crisp, vivid,
as if the season has flooded the day,
as if the day itself is a living thing.

IV.

The Baby

I.

Flaking paint in November air,
the house not what it was
when his wife lived, keeping watch.

Jacks and kings, queens,
tossed, shuffled and folded
for coins. "No women,"

Stefanos says, when a daughter
sets down her stack of bills
and her beer. This is no rule,

this is no law. It is truth.
He has six daughters, a son
who never married. None of his nine

grandchildren bear his name,
none speak Greek, the language
of his childhood, the language

of the newspapers stacked on the chair
in the corner of the kitchen....
Men around a table. The stakes:

quarter-half. Soon, blindness
and senility will take even this away.

II.

The daughters sing. Some silently,
some in Northern cities,
some together, echoing,

revising, their tongue American,
their tale Greek—rocky hills
of Karea, north of Gythion.

Begin at the beginning,
and she does. Her black skirts
clutched, her sandled feet,

red with cold, step over
roots, climb the hill
above the Massachusetts town

and its defunct factory.
Later, the Thanksgiving feast,
but now, the story:

I was twenty-one,
my first trip to Greece
driving with my father and mother.

Imagine me! Not yet married
hearing this....
It was his first trip back—

dirt roads with potholes,
we'd pass sheep, goats,
wild dogs. Breeze cool

through the window. It begins,
around 1920, in Karea,
a village of sixty people

in southern Greece. It begins with
my grandmother, my yiayia,
Ianthe.

III.

Her house was furthest from the well
at the foot of the village that stretched
up the mountainside.

The distance from the well,
the uphill walk, a sign
of poverty, yet when she looked

from her doorway toward the south,
there were no other houses,
no other people, only

the far off sea flashing between
two mountains, some days
white as blindness, some days a blue

sharp as a broken promise.
Was it blessing or curse
to live there? Where everyone

could see her, where she
        could see no one—so far
                from the well, so close

to the road.

IV.

She never told anyone, but,
        in her last years, Ianthe
                came to believe the shepherd

was not a shepherd, but
        Dionysius, disguised,
                some pagan energy.

It was late in the year,
        the figs had fallen, her husband,
                Kostas, still in America,

and a cool wind passed
        through her hut. She sent
                her boys for water

and they obeyed, not looking
        at him. She refused his drink.
                but held him when he took her.

She had waited six years
        for Kostas, while he gambled
                her fare to the States

in tenement poker games.
And now, this bronzed man,
younger, wanting her, his chest

broad, yet with few hairs,
like a boy's, spilling his wine
on her woven rug,

licking her breast.
When Stefanos returned,
pulling his young brother,

Yannis, with one hand,
the other carrying the water,
sloshing in its bucket,

his mother kissed his forehead
and thanked him. The rug,
Stefanos saw, had been turned.

V.

Just as it was his secret
in his own house,
years later, as his daughters

grew around him like wildflowers,
their songs changing
from Greek to English,

for his mother, Ianthe,
the child remained her secret,
her burden, her terror.

Just as, years later, awake
in the cold night, Stefanos did not know
whom to hate: his mother,

the shepherd, his father, she hated
herself, she hated the man,
she hated Kostas for his absence.

She hated the sheep
lowing on the mountainside,
the red streaks in the heavens,

and the visits of her uncle,
his mustache twitching as he ate,
wiping the corner of his lips

with his thumb and licking it. She hated
the frightened look on Stefanos' face,
as he sat outside the hut,

watching the road to Gythion,
to the sea, to America.

VI.

Like the breeze that carries
the scent of rain, the chill
gust that makes the animals

jittery, the dogs bark and leap:
suspicion. Her belly,
a swelling cloud. The men

stared into her eyes,
the women would not look at all.
Stefanos beat the lambs

harder. Yannis wailed for milk,
drooling on his chest.

VII.

Out of the hills he came:
a traveling priest, one
only interested in God's word.

The villagers fed him, listened
to his stories of the city.
He gave sweets to the children

before he spoke of her. He said
he'd heard in a nearby village
that a woman in Karea

had sinned, yet she was still
among them. He poured the men
some of his wine—the best they'd

ever tasted—"Is this true?" he asked.
The next morning, before the fog
below had lifted, when the road

to Gythion disappeared
into grey mist, they marched
to her house, pulled her from her fire

into the winter sun. Her uncle
stood in the doorway, blocking
the two boys inside, and ordered them

to lie in their beds
and cover their ears.
But when they pinned her to the earth,

the black cloth tightened over
her belly, and the priest saw
the slight rise, and knew. Before

her uncle could draw his knife,
the priest spoke of God's mercy,
then slapped her, ordered her gone.

There would be no murder.
The villagers, teeth bared, hands
hung with stones, shouted, threw at her

as she went to the door of her house
and called for her boys. They
wriggled past her uncle's legs

to hers. The stones kept coming.
One, then another, hit Yannis,
and he screamed and ran ahead,

stumbling over the rock and brush.
"Stefanos, Yannis," his uncle called.
"You don't have to go. Live

with me." A stone hit
his mother's shoulder, then
glanced off his and struck

his cheek. He ran, following
Yannis. Ianthe walked slowly
after them, as if to let

the village punish her
as thoroughly as it wished.

VIII.

"*Did she have the baby?*
What happened to it? Was the baby
his brother who died?"

"*No. Yannis was the brother who died,*
the one his father, Kostas, never saw.
He sailed before the birth."

When Yannis died of t.b.
at 19, in Athens, before
he could escape the army's

call and follow Stefanos to America,
Kostas sent a hundred dollars
for the funeral, or he said

he sent it. It never arrived,
and Ianthe buried him with money
collected quietly by Gythion neighbors

as poor as she. She never
asked for help. For her, people
meant whispers, and whispers meant

hate, and banishment, and so
when the two aging mothers handed her
the wooden box of bills and coin,

and told her which undertaker
would not cheat her, she could not
bring herself to thank them.

"Yes," she kept saying to their words.
"Yes." They left, thinking her lost
in grief.

IX.

Before the baby came, before
she moved to the basement room
in Gythion and cleaned

outhouses to survive,
she stayed in an abandoned shed
on the back of the mountain

where she could not see the sea.
The nights glowed with starlight,
and she would sit outside,

spring bristling invisible,
Stefanos curled against her humped belly,
Yannis asleep inside, sweat drying

in his black ringlets.
The mountains rose like gods—
no, she thought, like teeth.

She was inside a mouth, the breeze,
breath. She was sitting
on a great tongue, a silenced tongue,

a dry tongue, but still alive—
the breeze rushing through
her hair. "Mama,"—

and in Stefanos' voice
(she had thought him asleep)
a question: *Why?* And, *What now?*

She sighs, shifts her weight, and kisses
his head. His hand rises from his lap
to her belly, and he feels it

moving, he feels it, like
a lamb jerking as it's led
to slaughter, a tongue pushing,

lashing, inside a cheek.

X.

At the news of another
Greek who came over, someone
about the right age,

the sister who never left home
says, as she always says,
sitting at the head of the table,

the *Worcester Telegram* spread
before her, magnifying glass
in her hand, "Maybe

that's the baby." Stefanos
shivers, as he always does.
His wife dead last summer,

his mother dead ten years,
his father, twenty-five.
Maybe that's the baby.

He hates it. He hates this—
this foolishness, his daughter
thinking it only a matter of time,

of matching the dates, before
the baby appears. What does she
know of Greece, she, whose own Greek

is now worse than his English?
She has not stopped, she's doing
the math. Why had he told them?

To remind them of honor,
the value of virginity.
But since he has told them, why not

tell them the rest: "Stop!"
and "Stop!" again. He takes his glasses
in his hands. "The baby's dead."

XI.

He did not know the man, only
that he breathed wine
and was not cruel to his mother.

They left the shed, climbed
a nearby ridge,
Ianthe stopping and bending

low with each contraction,
her almost silent moans.
The man, erect, not looking,

not speaking, as if he didn't
comprehend pain, his chin
tilted uphill. A stable:

unused, forgotten, dusty.
"Stefanos," she said. "Yannis,
you stay outside,"

and she went in, and Stefanos
saw her knees fold
like a calf's, "Close

the door," she said to the man,
but it was as if he didn't
understand—why keep

it hidden? Down the slope,
Yannis was climbing a boulder,
and Stefanos wanted to join him

but he also wanted to stay,
to know, to see through the unclosed
doorway, to lie beside

his mother. Steel. The longest
blade he'd ever seen, appeared
in the man's hand, and Stefanos

went down to the rocks. He heard
his mother cry and stopped
moving. The cry wound down

the mountain like a rivulet,
around boulders and under bushes,
coating Stefanos's feet, flooding

through the rips in his shoes,
and then, more cries, hers,
then the newborn's, the current

rough, then weak, then dry
in the sun's late glare,
and Yannis digging with a stick

humming the lullaby that Ianthe
had sung to them last night.

XII.

Too fast, the cars fishtail
around the corner as Stefanos
sits on his porch, the first three

of his seven children obediently
inside the white fence, kicking
a ball, playing in English

and Greek. His father, Kostas,
sits, too, smoking, despite the heat.
He had driven down from Lowell.

The question hangs in the afternoon,
thickening like the grey paint
drying on the porch rails. He'd coated

them three times this morning.
He cannot ask it: *Why didn't you*
send for us? Just like he cannot

tell even his wife about the man
and the blade. Kostas spits the word
"whore," mutters "sorry." Years

later, a Christmas in New York City
at his daughter's 36th floor condo,
the table cleared after dinner,

coffee cup on a saucer in front of him,
he explains that afternoon—their voices
flinging accusations in Greek,

the children, ordered inside, faces
at the window, the clang of the church bells
on the hour, like blows pounding Sunday—

in two words: "We fight."

XIII.

After church, Ianthe spends her Sundays
at Stefanos', speaks loud, cranky Greek
with her daughter-in-law, draws

her hardened fingers down
a great-grandson's cheek,
their tips so worn they're smooth

("like a baby," they would say
in this country), as if even
the fingerprints' ridges—

those miniscule mountains—
have gone, lost to years working
the factory's lathe. Look,

look! How glossy, how worn.
They may have held a story once,
but in this Webster kitchen

there are no lines to read.

XIV.

Not quite five feet, hunched,
still in mourning black twelve years
after Kostas died. She speaks

no English, lives down the street
from Stefanos, the second floor
of a wooden triple-decker,

keeps a small garden in the back lot,
an oasis in the weedy, glassy sand.
Her left hand is missing its

last two fingers, no place to put
a wedding ring, no pinkie. Did she
lose them in the factory,

or was it something before
she crossed the Atlantic? She smells
of the bread she bakes, flour clouds

her black skirts grey. Glasses
cover her wrinkled face, darkened,
ages ago, by the Mediterranean sun.

She frightens her great-grandchildren
when she takes their chins
in her hand, squeezes, and kisses

their cheek, their forehead.
At her funeral, none come.

XV.

There was a knife.
    There was an infant.
        There was a man.

And there was a woman.
    And after, there was blood
        pooled on the dirt floor

and the woman—his mother—
    not sobbing, not even speaking,
        shiny-eyed, as if about

to set out on a long journey,
    which they did, the next day,
        walking nine miles to Gythion

and the sea, nine miles
    along the cart path, down
        the mountain's switchbacks,

Stefanos and Yannis playing
    number games: How many steps
        to that boulder? To the walnut tree?

XVI.

There were nights
    in the summer heat
        in her Webster flat

when she dreamed of him.
          Me, and a god!
                    she thought, *there, in my house.*

In her house, at the foot
          of Karea, her sons' voices faint,
                    then gone in the moans and the crackling

of the straw mattress. *And I—*
          she thought, touching, then rubbing
                    where he had been til in that small

bedroom the size of her stone house
          she had a spasm of ecstasy—
                    I bore a god's child.

And her fingers, her three fingers,
          traveled a last circle
                    round her sex, her eyes opened

and a car squealed, taking the corner
          too fast. Across the alley
                    Puerto Rican salsa banged the night.

XVII.

Stefanos gave his daughters
          fragments, but took his story
                    with him when he finally

folded into death at ninety, just as
          Ianthe took hers to her death.
                    All her mumbling beneath

her black veil, gone. Words,
Greek words, and sometimes
simply sound, song, music made

of the stones' rattle and thud,
Kostas' curses and lies, the cheap
wooden coffin for Yannis—

the heave of the Mediterranean,
the Atlantic, gone. Something
less than memory remains: the shadowed

doorway to the stable, the spring sun,
the dry wind passing through.

Made in the USA
Columbia, SC
26 October 2017